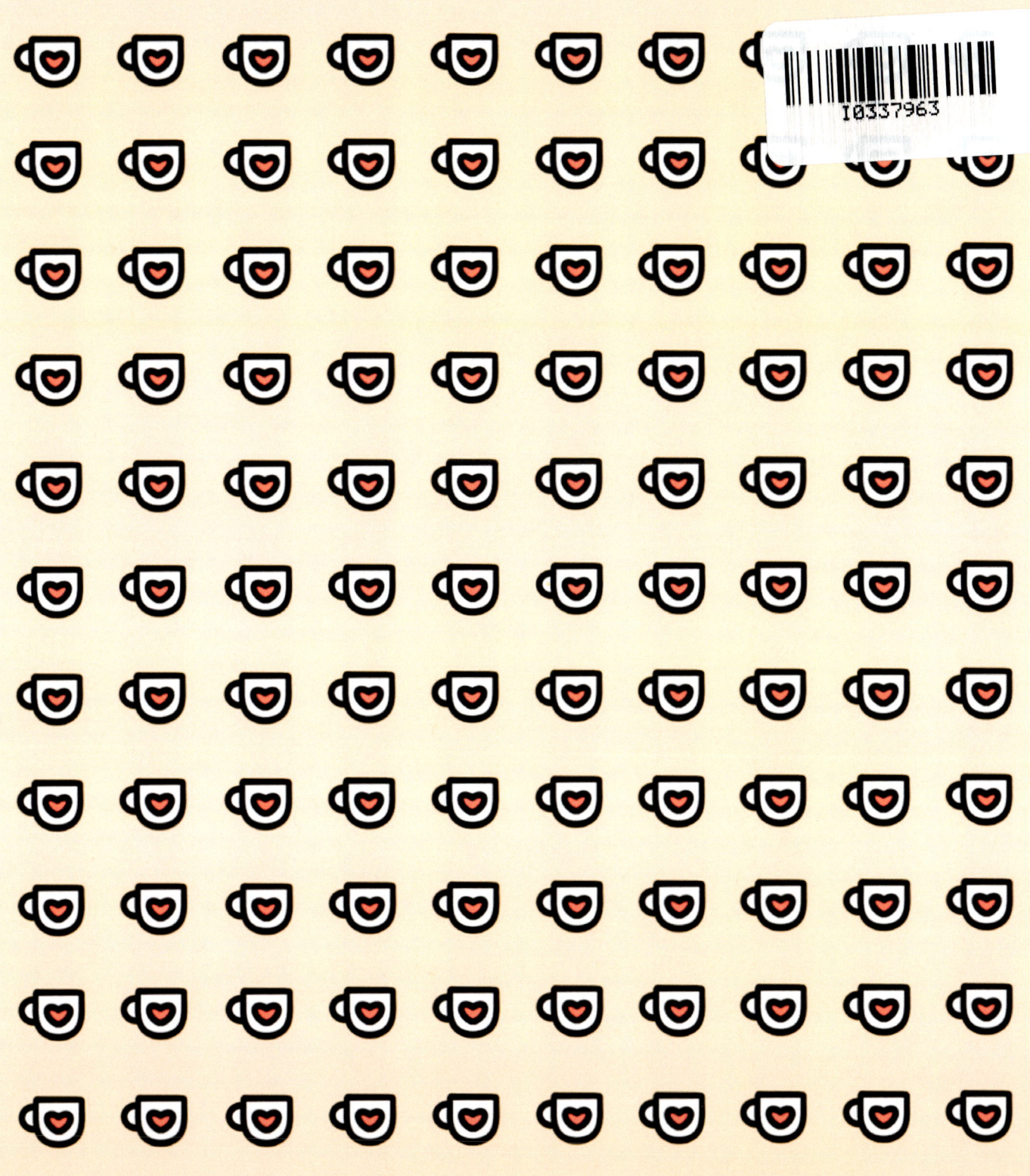

Chai Love You Very Much

Chai Love You Very Much

Written and illustrated by Joshveena Thirukonda Jholl

Copyright © 2024 Jhollygoodtimes

All rights reserved. No part of this book may be reproduced without written permission from the publisher.

First printed in July 2024

Published by Jhollygoodtimes
www.jhollygoodtimes.com

ISBN 978-0-6486142-2-7

This book belongs to

_____

I am a Chaiwala,

 I am a Chaiwali

and this is our chai shop.

We are ready to take your order

and promise our chai will be tip top!

First we bring the water, milk, masala and tea bags to boil in a pot.

once it's ready, the chai will be garma garam hot!

From cardamom to cloves,

cinnamon and ginger too..

There are lots of spices to choose from for the masala,

let us know if you want to try something new!

Different chais are available, please take your pick:

(Or we have filter coffee too, if that will do the trick)!

 Condensed milk,

 sugar,

 honey,

 sweetener

or nothing more if you please,

There is  morning,  afternoon,  evening

and special occasion chai to share

♡ with someone else or just yourself, ♡ for some ♡ tender loving chai care. ♡

Pakora

or curry puff?

www.ingramcontent.com/pod-product-compliance
Lightning Source LLC
Chambersburg PA
CBRC092340290426
44109CB00008B/172